Witness

POEMS TO ADDRESS THE PAST, PRESENT, AND FUTURE OF POLICING

EDITED BY
ARI TISON and TY CHAPMAN

WITH ARTWORK BY
DAMON DAVIS

ZEST BOOKS
MINNEAPOLIS

Contents

Letter from the Editors

Dear Reader,

If there's one thing we know as writers and poets, it's that the world is multifaceted. Some days pain sits by itself; other times it might be felt alongside joy. We know you know this too.

In our pain, we want to better our world. Sometimes we cast our votes to change policies and laws. And other times, we make our voices heard through protest. Still, in other times, we turn to poets, whose job it is to pay attention to the world, to bear memory to our histories, to see our realities, and to imagine new possibilities.

Poetry is one of the ways we can bear *witness*. In this collection, poets raise questions, poets mourn and lament, and poets dream. Poets bring their identities and life experiences to their writing, much as you bring your own background and life experiences to the page.

In gathering these poems, our goal is not to tell you what to think. Rather, we hope this anthology enters us into a conversation about policing—its history, its current reality, its variety of avenues—as well as possible alternative futures through a few dives into futurism.

Like you, we want to do our part in making this world a more beautiful place. Writing is one of the ways that we can.

But it doesn't just take a poet, it takes a reader too.

Here is your invitation to *witness*.

—Ari Tison & Ty Chapman

Speaking in the Silence

CAROLYN HOLBROOK

Coltrane's spirit calls "Life, life, and love"
I feel you, my brothers
I feel you, my sister
I feel you, my mother, my father
I feel you, my son

the ancestors stand beside me
and behind me
pushing me gently forward

I want to hear your stories

speak to me
speak through me
let me be a conduit
bring past into present
and future

let quiet speak
let the arms of those
who push me forward
lead me
toward love
toward peace
through the
rocking, humming, healing
our past

moving us toward love
toward life

No Kinda Right

NIKKI GRIMES

A simple violation, really:
overdue registration.
A change of address meant
I never got the notice—
an innocent enough mistake,
but would it be my last?

The police car lights behind me
send shivers screaming up my spine—

shivers centuries old, if truth be told,
terror burned into my bloodline.
Another melanin-skinned human
instantly afraid at the sight
of that particular blue,
seethes because there's reason.

"Protect and serve?" Please!
"Peace Officer?" A misnomer, at best.

Astronomical is the number of times
the lips of the earth have been ripped apart
so that she could be forced to drink
the blood of Black innocents
gone at the hand of some man in blue.

The white officer leans into my window.
Breathe, breathe, I tell myself,

wordlessly commanding my body
not to move a muscle.

"Yes sir. No sir. I will sir,"
is as much as I can manage.

Grateful to drive off, ticket in hand
and—Lord have mercy—Alive,
I grip the steering wheel
as rage rises in me, a steaming cauldron.
Hours pass before the terror
—unfairly bequeathed to me—subsides.

The Human Hand Has 27 Bones

At the Smith & Wesson Gallery of Firearms History, Springfield, Massachusetts

SUN YUNG SHIN

In the gray glass, I am a white man, *no*, a cowboy,
no, a soldier, *no*, a policeman. *Yes. I think I've said yes before.*

Inside the display, four neat pairs of handcuffs, used and worn,
dented and dinged. The bottom set, iron, rust, thick round shackles,

two locking bars, bracelets curved, curved like a wrist, like protection.
The newest pair is thin, bright, a short chain joining two circles.
Almost abstract.

A circle looks innocent, maternal.
What have your hands done? What will your hands do?
To the right, three police batons hang vertically,
as if held by invisible fingers. *Nightsticks.*

Billy clubs or *riot sticks*. Scuffed and scored,
handles lathed with concentric ridges.
A good grip. "Early batons were often made
by local area cabinetmakers." A skill, a craft.

Remember: Living trees know desire. Even dead wood has a long memory—
children learn that tree rings are calendars of thirst,
revealed by a long, deep cut.
Chop not split. *Does blood*

wash out of wood? Here, in the glass case, two longer batons
have leather thongs, loose loops, tied.
A hand must be tethered. *You are surely the Law.*

Parry, block, short swing, back swing, jab, crack:
it's all in the wrist.

27
DD 2025

Last Words

D. R. BERNSTROM

1.
He did not ride the BART to die!
When bullet pierced, he did not cry,
but said, with frantic, searching eyes
and breath as fragile as a sigh:
"You shot me. You shot me."

2.
Oscar Julias Grant, the Third–
from gasping mouth spilled bloody words,
words no officer should have heard,
words that slurred as vision blurred:
"You shot me. I got a four-year-old daughter. You shot me."

3.
"Amazing Grace, how sweet the sound!"
He sang slave-song while young but found
a slave he was, thrown down and bound,
and in his blood, destined to drown.
"You shot me, bruh. You shot me."

4.
"All we like sheep have gone astray,"
Lay down your stones for we've all strayed,
but he was put to death that day.
Could there have been no other way?
"You shot me, man. You shot me."

5.
Pain, fear, sorrow, hopes, crushed dreaming.
Black hearts breaking, numb with feeling.
"I have a daughter. a daughter. A DAUGHTER!"
BANG!
Oscar,
still,
no longer
reeling.
Mom and child left torn and screaming:
"You. shot. me. You. Shot . . . me."

6.
His favorite hue now marks the spot
his visage haunts where he was shot
Fruitvale Station. A mark, a plot
upon this road his name forced, wrought.

"You.
Shot.
Me.
Man.
You.
Shot . . .

FRUITVALE

BART

I Don't Know Where He Kept His Gun, with Headlines

LAURA RUBY

He wanted to adopt us long before he did, this man,
my mother's second husband. Wayward son of a
Cop who tased suspect several times
as man begged him to stop
violent drunk, he played football in college, ran off
the field after two semesters to enlist in the army.
Who was Rodney King? His 1991 beating
by L.A. police roiled America
I don't know where he kept his gun. Years later, he
braved wrecking balls, danced on girders alongside
123 Black people killed by white police officers
in one Alabama county
Indigenous ironworkers building bridges in New York
City. Dogs and horses, even cats, followed him everywhere.
After a failed police response to the shooting
deaths of 19 students and two teachers
in Uvalde, Texas, there were calls
for accountability
He believed in steel, in law and order. Finished a degree
in criminal justice, joined the police force. I don't know
Why . . . so many police traffic stops
turn deadly
where he stored his gun. He had a genetic condition that left
him without knuckles on both hands, an extra-thick skull, a
gulf remains between the public perception
of police violence and
how it is treated in court
jaw that could take any punch. Or so I thought. I don't
know where he locked his gun. A bit too tan to be white,
Leonard Cure, 53, exonerated after being
wrongly convicted of robbing a drug store in 2003,
killed after traffic stop in Georgia

nose strong enough to hook a twisted man's suspicions,
he was stopped himself, ordered to exit the vehicle,

Bodycam records officer saying a woman run over
by Seattle police had "limited value"

obey instructions. Informed they had probable
cause. For anything. He told me if the cops

killed Dexter Wade with a car, buried him,
didn't tell his mother for months

had a legal right to beat Rodney King, they had no moral
one. Said it was an officer's duty to de-escalate, defuse.

Police taser school band director
at US football game

He said half the people join the police to serve and protect,
while the others are a-holes on a power trip. I don't know

A year after the Uvalde massacre:
did anything change?

where he sold his gun. He quit the force to drive a delivery truck.
He drove until his memory went, until those bones could not

As the violence escalated, King issued
a plea: "Can we all get along?"

absorb another punch. He's gone now, my father. Dogs
and horses followed him everywhere, maybe they follow

Few police officers who cause deaths
are charged or convicted

still. Wayward son. I don't know if he ever pulled
his gun. I don't know when. Where. I don't know

How a false tale of police heroism . . . spread
and unraveled. The officer has since been
released on bond.

With language gathered from ABC News, *The Washington Post*, Northeastern Global News, *The New York Times*, BBC News, *The Guardian*, NBC News, AL.com, and *El Paso Times*.

Breath Under Water

KAO KALIA YANG

When the fishing boat toppled underneath the lift bridge,
perhaps the Hmong man saw a door open in the mouth of the dragon.

"Listen," the dragon could have said.
"I know the fears you've carried across oceans."

The rain that fell from the sky that day continued to fall long into the night.
Ripples big and small across the surface of the rushing river,
breath under water, breath under water.

Years later, another Hmong man drives across the same lift bridge.
Two girls sit in the back seat of his car, their bangs straight lines
across round eyes.

He tells them, "Right under this bridge is where Yia died. He was fishing.
He was a good swimmer. We couldn't find his body. The police said
they'd done all they could do. Something got him. Maybe a dragon.
Dragons lurk in these waters."

Caught in the words, the children do not notice the droplets
coming from the sky.
They do not pay attention to how the rain weeps
on the windshield of the car.

It is the sound of sirens that jerk them away from the voice of their father,
away from the story of the Hmong man who disappeared
in the waters below them,
and the dragon that waits beneath the surface of everything.

The day has darkened.
Flashing lights from a metallic head.

"Stay in the car, keep your hands where I can see them!" a voice shouts.

That which they feared, that which they had carried across oceans,
alive and well.

The dead Hmong man in the story of the fishing boat toppling in the water,
memory rising from the fog of the river, turns to mist.

The younger girl, hand to the cold glass, stares at the single eye of a badge.

Below the river rushes, and ripples form across the surface,
breath under water, breath under water.

They tried to bury the neighborhood

For the Twin Cities

TY CHAPMAN

but ain't we still here?

Stubborn & lovely, so many
dandelions sprouting fuzzy heads,
catching wind & drifting skylines.
Ain't they try to sunder bud from stem?
To pave lands we grow from—fragment
& border—bury all that's soft & giving?

Ain't we still here?

Corralled by crosswalks: high rises & I-94—
ain't there more granola spots than ma shops in soil
we made roots? Ain't dirt we sprang from turning
dry? Bitter & stingy, don't it take more than give?
Names drifting 'tween breezes, autumn leaves.
Brought from distant land, then offed. Wigs blown back
still budding for false prophecies. Spectracide
boys, good & old, wilt groves to patches.

But ain't we still here?

Blooming through potholes, reaching for sun-
touched skylines. Digging toes in earth that's soft
& giving. Ain't the elders teach us how
to lay new roots? Digging deep & spreading,
coupling networks spell:
Floydtown, Castileland, Wrightville.
Pavement cracked & buckling.
New growth surging for fresh air.

Ain't we still here?

See You Tomorrow

ERIN ENTRADA KELLY

There is a world
where an old man totters
toward his grandchildren,
pinches their cheeks,
pretends to steal their noses,
says, *My, how you've grown!*
or maybe he does none of those things
because he's a different type—
get off my lawn and
turn that down and
when I was your age—
or maybe he keeps to himself,
answers the phone when you call,
says, *I'm doing just fine,*
sits on his stoop,
waves to the neighbors,
keeps the thermostat high,
and maybe he has a favorite treat—
cinnamon drops or Tootsie Rolls—
and a favorite place to make groceries
and the cashiers love him;
they say, *Hey, Mr. Castile,*
all friendly and familiar-like
and they say *see you tomorrow*
and he waves over his shoulder
and they think, *oh, the stories he must have,*
and maybe he loves to tell them,

an old man with endless tales
going on and on about this and that,
about his grandson's new job
about his great-grandbaby's dance recital
and how she had more attitude than
anyone else on the stage
and that makes him laugh—
a good, aged laugh—
and you can't help but laugh too
even though you've heard it a dozen times,
but one story he never tells
is when he was pulled over by police
on a warm summer night in July;
that day was so insignificant,
license and registration, nothing more,
mundane even, not worth remembering,
forgotten long ago.

A New National Anthem

ADA LIMÓN

The truth is, I've never cared for the National
Anthem. If you think about it, it's not a good
song. Too high for most of us with "the rockets'
red glare" and then there are the bombs.
(Always, always, there is war and bombs.)
Once, I sang it at homecoming and threw
even the tenacious high school band off key.
But the song didn't mean anything, just a call
to the field, something to get through before
the pummeling of youth. And what of the stanzas
we never sing, the third that mentions "no refuge
could save the hireling and the slave"? Perhaps
the truth is every song of this country
has an unsung third stanza, something brutal
snaking underneath us as we absentmindedly sing
the high notes with a beer sloshing in the stands
hoping our team wins. Don't get me wrong, I do
like the flag, how it undulates in the wind
like water, elemental, and best when it's humbled,
brought to its knees, clung to by someone who
has lost everything, when it's not a weapon,

when it flickers, when it folds up so perfectly
you can keep it until it's needed, until you can
love it again, until the song in your mouth feels
like sustenance, a song where the notes are sung
by even the ageless woods, the shortgrass plains,
the Red River Gorge, the fistful of land left
unpoisoned, that song that's our birthright,
that's sung in silence when it's too hard to go on,
that sounds like someone's rough fingers weaving
into another's, that sounds like a match being lit
in an endless cave, the song that says my bones
are your bones, and your bones are my bones,
and isn't that enough?

This Has Always Been Our Active Shooter Drill

JASON REYNOLDS

(for Stephon Clark's grandmother)

shave your face. a haircut
even. kiss your kids. your
partner. your parents. tell
them you listened. you kissed
their asses like you were
taught. kissed their asses and
still. walk. or run. don't
matter. glue your identification
to your forehead. wrap yourself
in the flag. hand over heart. hit
the high note. hide your slang
under your tongue. delete
your profile. scrub the net. clean
your blood. prepare your body
for peepholes no one
will ever peer into.

THE REBEL POETS

Can we please give the police department to the grandmothers?

JUNAUDA PETRUS

Can we please give the police departments to the grandmothers? Give them the salaries and the pensions and the city vehicles, but make them a fleet of vintage Corvettes, Jaguars, and Cadillacs, with white leather interiors. Convertibles. Digging the scene with the gangsta lean.

Let the grandmas' squad cars be badass!

You would hear the old-school jams like Patti LaBelle, Stevie Wonder, Anita Baker, and Al Green. You would hear Sweet Honey in the Rock harmonizing on "We who believe in freedom cannot rest" bumping out the speakers.

And they got the booming system.

If you up to mischief, they will pick you up swiftly in their sweet rides and look at you until you catch shame. She will ask you if you are hungry and you say yes and of course you are. On the dashboard you will see brown faces like yours, shea-buttered and loved up.

And there will be no precincts.

Just love temples with spaces to meditate and eat delicious food. Mangoes, blueberries, nectarines, cornbread, peas and rice, fried plantain, fufu, yams, greens, okra, pecan pie, salad, and lemonade.

Things that will make your mouth water and soul arrive.

All the hungry bellies know warmth. All the children will expect love. The grandmas help you with homework, practice yoga with you, and teach you how to make jambalaya and coconut cake. From scratch.

When you're sleepy a grandma will start humming and rub your back while you drift off. A song that she used to have the record of when she was your age. She remembers how it felt like to be you and be young and not know the world that good. Grandma is a sacred child herself—one who's just circled the sun enough times to enter into the ripeness of her cronehood.

She wants your life to be sweeter.

When you are wildin' out because your heart is broke or you don't have what you need, a grandma will take your hand and lead you to her gardens. You can lie down amongst the flowers. Her grasses, roses, dahlias, irises, lilies, collards, kale, eggplants, blackberries. She wants you to know that you are safe and protected, limitless, sacred, sensual, divine, and free.

The grandmas are the original warriors, wild since birth, comfortable in loving fiercely. They have fought so that you don't have to, not in the same ways at least.

So give the police departments to the grandmas. They are fearless, classy, and actualized. Blossomed from love. They wear what they want and say what they please.

Believe that.

There won't be noise citations when the grandmas ride through our streets, blasting Erykah Badu, Nina Simone, Marvin Gaye, Alice Coltrane, Jimi Hendrix, KRS-One. All that good music. The kids gonna hula-hoop to it and sell them lemonade made from heirloom pink lemons and maple syrup. The cars will be solar powered with no carbon footprints—the grandmas designed the technology themselves.

At night the grandmas will park the cars in a circle so that all can sit in them with the tops down. You'll look at the stars, talk about astrological signs and what to plant tomorrow based on the moon's mood. They will help you memorize Audre Lorde and James Baldwin quotes. A grandma will always look you in the eye and acknowledge the light in you with no hesitation. She loves you fiercely forever.

The grandmothers see the pain in our bravado, the confusion in our anger, the depth behind our coldness. Grandma knows what oppression has done to our souls and is gonna change it one love temple at a time.

The grandmothers have no fear.

OD IS

Church

ARI TISON

It wasn't when my mother left me, or my father died. It wasn't when the wind snapped the trees around my childhood house. We mourned for those trees for days. No, it wasn't even when that man kept breaking into my room. No, it was when I woke up & I could smell the ash through my open windows. When I couldn't watch the video. I couldn't pray, lying on the floor. I couldn't protest, not to God or others. I didn't go places because if we left, we wondered if we'd make it home. Some of my friends almost got ran over by a semi. I couldn't pray for weeks when the entire world had things to say. Not until I woke up early, went to the corner at Cup Foods. My home neighborhood. The humidity of the bodies who had been there the last night lingered. The ground near empty, someone meditating, another clearing wilted flowers. Then I stood at the bus stop & could see where he reached out. He prayed for people, they say. Inside the bus stop walls was stained glass of glued-on voices, pasted in every color, the light of the morning coming through. Voices grasping & I was brought to church.

What to say to God? That same officer was cruel to my friend.
That my dad knew George's girlfriend.
That witness—was a wrestling coach, & his team competed against my nephew's—could tell you now I saw him a year later helping some kids on the side of the road. A woman in a Suburban parked ahead. When I drove by, he & I nodded at each other.

My soul cracked open that day in a place of transience. Too much transience. I couldn't pray until I heard us home people crying from the walls themselves. Feel our weeping soaked into the heavy air. They had made for me a bus stop, a church bench, a spot to sit long enough to remember who God is near for anyway.

T
5
BUS STOP
1 HR PARKING
HEAT, SPARK
Flame
Not everything that is faced can be changed But nothing can be changed until it is faced
Justice Now!
MY Cries ARE 4 humaniTY
Justice for GEORGE

WESTERN
Arrest them ALL!!!
ONLY COWARDS KILL THE UNARMED
BLACK LIVES MATTER
RIP GEORGE FLOYD
WATCH US WE fight for you to See The change From above
George FLOYD
full of Life
JUSTICE for GEORGE FLOYD
PEACE
STOP YNCHING US
WE ♡ & HONOR YOU GEORGE I AM SORRY PLEASE FORGIVE US
MY LIFE MATTERS
we remember
I CAN'T BREATHE
REST IN POWER ORGE FLOYD

Without Context

PADMA VENKATRAMAN

Caught like tattered cloth on the barbed wire of memory
I'm sometimes an unmoored immigrant girl once more
alone, on my own, in a new country,
learning to drive, struggling to live on a student's salary.
Returning from the laboratory in my rusty car one rainy night,
I see pulsing blue light behind me.

Weeks ago, I pulled over for a tow truck's flashing yellow lights.
When I stopped feeling silly, I shared the story.
My labmates couldn't stop laughing.

This time, though, police. Definitely.
I stop. Not sure what to do next. Open the door? Get out?
No. Officer's already at my window, barking.
License and registration.
Are they in my bookbag? Or in the dash?
I start rummaging for my wallet.
Why's he so angry? I'm fumbling. Panicking.
Can't understand his American accent.
His hands crawl toward his hip holster.
Is he lifting—is that really a gun? Is this a joke?
How can he yell at me to get my license
but tell me to keep my hands on the wheel?

Surreal laughter—mine—cuts through the hiss of rain.
Time speeds up again. The policeman lowers his weapon.

His face I forget within minutes
but his pale-haired hands still shred my sleep.
And I can't forget stories of many who weren't as lucky as me.
Like Amadou Diallo, with his round, brown face, bright eyes,
and brows thick and straight and black as mine.
Amadou Diallo, twenty-three, immigrant from Guinea. See him:
smiling at his cousin, reaching for his wisp
of American dream, day after long day,
selling gloves and socks on a sidewalk
along 14th Street, shadowed by skyscrapers.
Hear excitement in his voice when he calls
his mother, Kadiatou, to say
he's finally saved enough to pay for college.
Amadou Diallo, about to achieve his hope,
unarmed, strolling home after a meal one cold winter evening,
reaching for his wallet, when NYPD police accost him,
then fire 41 times.
Because I'm a mother now, praying for my brown child's safety.
Because we share American nightmares.

Saturday Morning on 3rd and Lenora

TAE KELLER

Seattle is asleep
when we reach the corner,
dragging two small wagons full of
    not that much—
        blankets, hand warmers, gloves, hot cocoa
    and all the tents donations could buy—
like girl scouts with nothing to sell
and not enough to give.

The cold has teeth today.
And too, the police.
SPD circles the block slow,
readying for a sweep.

My partner says something
about bad apples.

On the sidewalk, a man steals
sleep like a crime,
  couldn't repay the debt
  gathered beneath his eyes.
He wakes as I pass, and when I offer
our dwindling supplies,
he accepts only coffee.

We pretend the police aren't circling.

In another life,
we're chatting in a café,
neighbors on Saturday—

But now as I pour hot water,
cold shakes me, knocking
shame from its perch.
I, mall-jeaned and weak,
clench my chattering teeth.
I think of biology,
freshman year, jaws
of early humans proved
a diet mostly fruit—
and what a useless thing to know
when the person in front of you
knows hunger.
The man palms the cup tender,
sips steam.
Don't be cold, he says.
Don't be cold.

It begins to snow.
The police exit their cars,
their teeth sharp
as guns.

Don't be cold, don't be cold.

At the end of the block,
they descend on sidewalk residents,
start bagging their belongings, stealing
as if theft isn't crime—
trashing the blankets we just gave out.

A woman walks toward me,
hands empty as a promise.
They took everything, she says.
I reach for her with a fistful of hand warmers—
        This is all we have left.
She stares.
Couldn't take all those, she says.
Wouldn't want to be greedy.
I empty my hands into hers.
        Please.

I am begging.

I am begging.

In another life, there are homes
and the price of life—
        there is no price.
Survival's free as a Saturday,
and the only apples grow on trees.
In another life trees grow bounty,
  Don't be cold,
        we won't be cold,
Because our teeth were made for orchards,
who needs a bite sharper
when the fruit is fresh for picking
   and we are reaching—

                we are reaching.

This Year, 29 Anti-Trans Bills Became Law

a contrapuntal

OLLIE SCHMINKEY

fear
this is nothing new, just
history that stirs my blood & simmers

i know fear best by the way
every time i go to the airport
i bare my teeth at the TSA agent, as if
my *girl* voice will
stop the pat down:
my pockets, my private body. i am
not the way they think i should be,
& safety is a game i play—
the last hundred & a half years,
we could have been arrested
& now Tennessee becomes a fist

for centuries,
my gender was
illegal
thousands of people
arrested, thrown in psych wards for
simply wearing clothes
this year, they hire cops at pride
& we all press the knife to
our own necks
our reflection
in the blade.
what is a knife if not
a mirror? what is
a gathering of trans people if not
a reason in itself to fear

joy
the sun on her skin, her fingers are golden
between my knuckles

i can't help but smile.
i unpeel my name,
my softness can protect me here—
turn my chest normal, but never
turn me inside out—
whole, i am a real person, just
the beginning of a laugh.
if only we could stop
time unfolding itself again
in the beauty of this moment,
exactly the size of my heart.

i wanted to be held just like this. like
the sun on a new leaf. love is newly
inside me most days. the world is
cheering as i am
loving myself
the only way that feels true,
& we travel back in time. i laugh
the music from my own good throat,
like a piñata broken open,
like confetti, our smiles dancing
what is love if not a song?
a new way to hold hands? what is history if not
the shortest way home? what is
a chosen family? what is love but
my own good joy.

Uvalde Villain-elle

K. A. HOLT

What else could they have done,
on that sunny spring day in Texas,
so busy they were, standing around and helping no one?

Three hundred and seventy of them stood in the sun,
waiting for eight agencies to coalesce—
what else could they have done?

They wanted to prepare; to ensure the fight was already won,
and yet they appeared feckless,
so busy they were, standing around and helping no one.

Three hundred and seventy law enforcement agents, overcome—
one man with one gun had rendered them helpless.
What else could they have done?

Then! Seventy-seven minutes after shot number one,
the good guys who protect us
were all done standing around and helping no one.

On my count, let's go! 3-2-1—
The heroes unlocked that classroom door, only to find 21 souls lifeless.
What else could they have done?
So busy they were, standing around and helping no one.

Watershed (A Scene from the Very Near Future)

KYLE TRAN MYHRE

We arrive at the press conference just in time to see the City reaching
over to shake hands with the robot officer with no hands. The City shakes.
The cameras flash. The City, standing so tall in the train station, so proud
of his sound bite: *the apples can't be rotten when they're made of steel.*

This is, of course, after the flood, and the other flood, and the other flood,
and the other flood. After we've traded our tiny basement apartment
for the even tinier corner of a cousin's living room. The City doesn't patch
the holes in its boots. The City doesn't spend money on improved drainage

systems, or rental assistance for families. The City hires a dozen new
robo-cops. Shiny and mindless, like rubber bullets the size of teenagers, like
gym rat R2-D2s in klan robes. The City takes a single reporter's question
but the scream of metal on metal is too much; all I hear is the repetition,

the same forced-smile-focus-grouped-concrete-language quip: *the apples
can't be rotten when they're made of steel.* Can't help but think the City
is forgetting something important about apples. Can already feel the teeth
loosening in my jaw, the ringing in the bite. Plant one of those in the ground

(a tooth, a seed from a steel apple, a man rolling his eyes) and see what
grows. The City departs, two assistants with black umbrellas battling
to shield the never-ending rain from his single little head. And then it's just
us and the empty egg, the million dollar sandbag. This is, of course, before

the City learns that you need a bunch of flesh cops to guard the robo-cop.
(*Who watches the watchmen?* indeed) We step forward. It just sits there,
not helping anyone or doing anything (such fidelity). We step forward.
It sees us through a camera. It hears us through a microphone. Always,

a border. Nothing new. Just progress. We step forward. A drone by any
other name. A litany of all the rights for which we should be grateful. We
step forward. Honestly . . . we were only there to heckle the thing. To take
pictures and post funny captions. And I don't believe in big, lightning

strike eureka moments, but I know: No one said anything clever. No one
took a picture. The difference between *full* and *flood* is a drop. We all felt it:
the question departing *how loud do we have to be to get its attention?*
and arriving *how hard do we have to push to knock it onto the tracks?*

“Designed for Off the Chain”
Call & Response Gorget

DOUGLAS KEARNEY

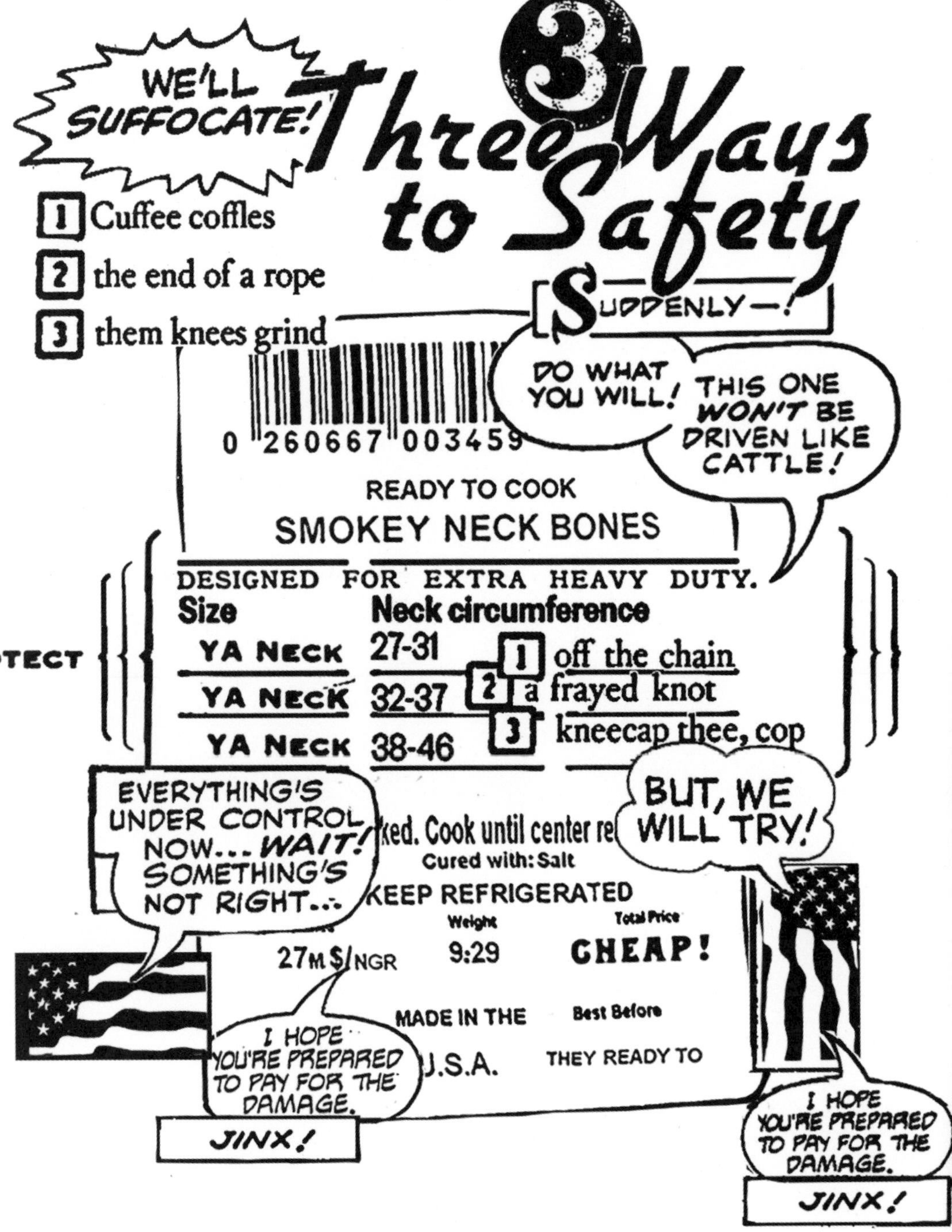

8 (9)

BAO PHI

In memory of Fong Lee;
and for the Lee family, and the Justice for Fong Lee committee

In 2006, Minneapolis Police Officer Jason Andersen shot and killed Fong Lee, a 19-year-old Hmong American. Andersen was awarded a Medal of Valor, though the Lee family and community members allege that Fong Lee was unarmed and the gun found on the scene was planted by police. During a foot chase in North Minneapolis, Andersen shot at Lee 9 times, 1 bullet missing, the other 8 hitting Fong Lee as he ran and as he lay dying on the ground.

1.
Community members point out that accusations about Fong Lee's history and character, specifically allegations that he was in a gang, were allowed in court and written about in the press. But Officer Andersen's alleged dislike of Asians and history of derogatory remarks against Asians was neither allowed in court nor written about in the press.

One of the devil's greatest powers
Is to force you to take a deal
That he himself would never take.

2.
Fong Lee was 19 (*gang member*). I can imagine him (*gang member*) and his (*gang member*) family. They are eating (*gang member*) something that steams, and it does not steam like food from this (*gang member*) country, the smell lingers (*gang member*) like home. It is Minnesota so (*gang member*) the lights inside no matter how dim somehow make (*gang member*) all indoor rooms feel warm. Now it's summer and he's fishing

with his (*gang member*) friends. They (*gang member*) get on bikes and their (*gang member*) legs drape low (*gang member*), arms lazy crosses on the handlebars. Their heads lean as they debate the Minnesota Vikings (*gang member*) and the Minnesota Twins, slapping absently at the logos (*gang member*) on their caps and (*gang member*) shirts.

3.

Officer Jason Andersen (*hero*) shot Hmong American teenager Fong Lee eight times (*to serve and protect*). A bullet wound in Fong Lee's hand suggests the teenager may have held his hands up in surrender (*decorated officer*) as Officer Andersen (*white*) shot (*Medal of Valor*) him. Andersen was also charged with domestic assault (*peace officer*) by his girlfriend though charges were later dropped (*officer of the law*). Officer Andersen (*police officer*) was also accused of kicking (*hero*) an African American teenager who was on the ground in handcuffs in 2008.

4.

An all-white jury found Officer Andersen not guilty of using excessive force.
Put a blindfold on me
Tell me who you fear
And I will tell you
Your skin.

5.

I'm wondering when people will care.
If we made your story into a movie about killing dolphins, perhaps.

6.
I'm 18 and the brutal cold holsters my hands into the warm solace of my jacket pockets. The police officer snaps his hand to his gun. My pockets are empty. My hands open. Still. My story would have ended in smoke and red snow. If my body lay there, perforated, would I bleed through holes in his story?

7.
Lost, you turn the car around and see trees stretching up like green-brown fencing up to the blue skies. For a moment you think that woods stretch forever, somewhere close a bubbling stream whispers white kisses across worn rocks, a deer leans its neck down to drink, the velvet moss of a hushed secret world here in your city. But just beyond the neck of scrub trees is the hint of chain-link, the distant ghost silhouette of strip mall, just one step past the shadows of those leaves are railroad tracks running like stitches over broken glass and gravel.

Minnesota Nice: this city hides its scars so well.

8.
All our lives, men with guns.
Chased, in the womb, in the arms
Of our parents.

Our parents
Chased, all our lives,
By men with guns.

In the womb, in our parents' arms
We've run
Chased by men with guns.

(9).
Michael Cho. Bich Cau Thi Tran. John T. Williams.
Tycel Nelson. Oscar Grant. Fong Lee.
May your names be the hymn
wind that sways
police bullets to miss.

The Policeman

JASMINE WARGA

The first time I saw Miró's painting *The Policeman,*
I didn't yet know about the concept of negative space,
or maybe I did know about it,
but I didn't *know* the word—
if you can't name it,
it doesn't exist,
right?

In *The Policeman,*
there is a human figure
and a figure of a horse.

I do not know if the man
and the horse are aligned
or if they are fighting.

Is the policeman trapping what is wild,
what they call uncivilized,
what they call barbaric?

Or has he already harnessed it,
made it his,
inverted and reverted and dispossessed?

But who cares about the man and the horse?

I am more interested in the void,
in the negative space,
what exists between the figures in the painting,
what is unnamed.

The day I first saw *The Policeman*
was a cold one

in the middle of an endless Midwest February.
My boots were leaking mushy snow
on the perfect polished wooden floors
and even though I was shivering,
I was remembering being thirteen,
and waiting to board a plane to Jordan,
which wasn't home,
which had never really been home,
but still,
we were going,
and
we were being questioned,
there were rules to follow,
and I didn't understand them,
or why only some people had to follow them,
and other people got to enforce them.

And then I'm thinking about being in the back
of the old car,
driving down the hills of Amman,
toward the border,
the invisible border,
the border with armed guards—

I am thinking about my American passport,
and how it lets me enter,
but my last name,
which makes the man with the gun
(who has an American accent himself)
pause and give me a look
that makes me think of the gun

and negative space.

I am thinking about the word police
and the word man
and how the word police
comes from the Latin word for state
and what is a state
and who gets to belong to the state
is determined
by the police.

Someone once told me
that if you trace the word
police back further,
you end up in ancient Greece,
thinking about cities
and what it means to be a citizen.
Why do some people who live in the city
not get to be citizens?

I have learned to police my own tongue
when it comes to explaining my citizenship—
my affiliation to my cities—
my affiliation to cities whose names have been erased—
scrubbed clean from maps.

I am American,
no really, American,
okay, my father is from—

pause   pause   pause
the space between figures
the negative
the liminal—

I do not name my father's real citizenship
I do not name the cities that have been

scrubbed
erased.

I tell myself it is because
it is complicated
hard
interrupted by war and dispossession

You know the word I don't say
the word that is fractious enough
to split this poem in two.

A word that defines
and defies negative space.

Imagine a word having the ability
to conjure feelings like that,
a word that is both
policed and possessed.

When I look at the painting these days,
I don't care much about the horse
or the policeman.

But I am drawn to the negative space
to the power of seeing it,
in saying its name,

in not letting it be
scrubbed
erased
possessed.

In English We Say

After Whitney Hanson

FONG LI BLESSING

In English we say: *stop resisting*

But in poetry we say:

Some people get to decide
Whether I return
To my warm home, or to
A rusty cellblock of concrete

Or whether to replace my bed with
A wooden box body-shaped
To rest for eternity.

Before blending my face
On concrete, knees on my neck—
See me.

The way I cut my hair, clean undercut
And the way I dress—baggy pants and
Shirts two sizes bigger.

Words my mother says when she is kind:
zoo nraug handsome.

See me,
Before you note the color of my skin
Before squeezing tight that metal circle
Around my wrists

Maybe then you could believe in my humanity.
Maybe then you would put your gun where it belongs.

Maybe then I wouldn't fear calling for help.

The Labor of a Dream

AIDA SALAZAR

We come from a long line of dreamers
Bracero blood braced itself
inside our veins
generations of the ebb
and go
run and
come back tumble
of migrant imaginings
for a better life
an un-violated life
a hunger-less life.

Abundance measured
by the cracks on
our dishpan hands
our book-filled hands
our toiling hands
our back broken hands
bounty in belly hearts full
despite Yankee spit on our faces
or the swollen echoes of "beaner"
bleached into our skin.

Grandfathers, grandmothers,
mothers, fathers,
children,
us
lawful before laws
abiding instead by the prophecy
that we'd wander back across
lands our ancestors once abandoned
survival etched into every impossible day
inside this US where we've

slept and awoken
to loves long lost
to customs
to family
to earth
between barbed wire
deserts and the greatness
of a river now red with our blood.

Our futures fade into longing
to stay, to ignore the mandate
to return to the place
where we are further unknown
where not all is pristine
like mountain
like spring
like memory.

We remain here,
deemed dreamers
denounced for dreaming
inside the vacuum of history, erased
we must yet again fight
for the light to be human
to tear open the minds of those
who wish to see us vanished
to rise
to be seen as citizen
to be read
as always having belonged.

This poem was written on Labor Day of 2017 as the US government deliberated over the fate of Deferred Action for Childhood Arrivals (DACA). If ended, eight hundred thousand registered undocumented immigrants stood to be deported.

On June 18, 2020, the United States Supreme Court upheld DACA by ruling that the Trump administration did not provide sufficient evidence for rescinding it.

Palabras y vida / Words and Life

MARGARITA ENGLE

"Patria y vida"
Homeland and Life
instead of the official slogan
patria o muerte
homeland or death.

It's easy to imagine
that the US is more merciful
than my ancestral Cuba
but while rappers, artists,
poets, and painters
were being arrested
en la isla
for singing
a protest song
about death versus la vida
about and versus or . . .

George Floyd called out for his mama,
then breathed his last life-loving words,
"They'll kill me."

Maykel Osorbo was already in prison in Cuba
when he received a Latin Grammy for the protest song
called "Patria y vida."

The title by itself, even without the power of music, is a protest
simply because it alters the old authoritarian slogan
"Patria o muerte"—"Homeland or death."

Life, not death.
And, not or.
Such brief words
can make
such a difference.
Hope, not despair.

Strict censorship on the island.
Racist book bans in the US.

Maykel Osorbo.
George Floyd.

Their mothers.

Or.
And.

My only consolation is knowing
that words can never be chained
or murdered.

Words escape.
Words survive.
Words fly.
Words are spirits
mamá, mama, vida, life, oye, listen, mira, watch
as our own palabras
words of protest

grow wings

and rise.

For Renee Nicole Good

Killed by I.C.E. on January 7, 2026

AMANDA GORMAN

They say she is no more,
That there her absence roars,
Blood-blown like a rose.
Iced wheels flinched & froze.
Now, bare riot of candles,
Dark fury of flowers,
Pure howling of hymns.

If for us she arose,
Somewhere, in the pitched deep of our grief,
Crouches our power,
The howl where we begin,
Straining upon the edge of the crooked crater
Of the worst of what we've been.

Change is only possible,
& all the greater,
When the labour
& bitter anger of our neighbors
Is moved by the love
& better angels of our nature.

What they call death & void
We know is breath & voice;
In the end, gorgeously,
Endures our enormity.

You could believe departed to be the dawn
When the blank night has so long stood.
But our bright-fled angels will never be fully gone,
When they forever are so fiercely Good.

The Harvest Destroys the Hive

KARUNA RIAZI

We're fighting for turf. We're fighting for the streets.

—Barbara Rothenberg, a DC real estate agent advocating for policing of Black bodies and their removal from the area in 1981

After so many late-night white flights, the district was left an empty hive—
    (a neighborhood in DC,
    The historical Hill in Pittsburgh,
    A street of brownstones in Brooklyn—
    The terrain doesn't matter, just the freed expanse,
    The abandoned possibility.)

And so, the workers moved in.

Ugly urban bones are now done up in rich honeycomb:
    houses set together in cozy neighborhood chambers,
    joyful song spilling from opulent theaters and open church doors.
And, even on the less decorated corners,
Where bodies follow scent trails to every viable
Stoplight and street corner,
Performing there the old dances of survival that
Are disdained for their desperation.
There is the dripping nectar of money
    (community, prosperity, unity)
that steeps into the walls,
Sets them firm,
Gives them worth.
And with worth comes want.

And if not want
    Envy.
There's nothing that aggravates more than the sight of success
In what was supposed to be disdained and discarded.

All
Cops
Are
Bludgeons brought down on the thriving hive.

Broken window policing smashes apart the honeycomb.
Greedy, grinding heel crushes enduring exoskeleton into sidewalk.
Seething, scornful wasps stamp out their new territories,
through real estate signs and newly rendered maps
imposed upon previously claimed boulevards and avenues.

Conquest, disguised as rightful harvest.

Banishment laws and bullets do the dirty work.

Gentrification leaves heavy gashes
where Black bodies have looked around urban decay
seeing where they can line a deserted street with
their own little chambers
fill them with the golden
        sunshine of hope
        manna of endurance—
can't let them have this turf
any more than a bear's claws will spare the worker bee's labor.

Empty, broken
—the human hive, the streets, the dreams.

Better for it?

So they claim.

A Broken Crown for Homeless Queer Youth

ALICE PAIGE

(I)

Iowa winter claws in contempt of my labored walk to a new school.
Snow—I can't stop writing about its falling.
The way a lonely county crouches beneath its own silence. Schoolboy
hands me a sack of mildewed clothes to replace the abandoned. Icicles
grow long in the tooth from poorly shingled roofs and another man arrives
to pound on a borrowed door. I stumble out of
my first shower in days to show him my ID. Yes, I am _____ and I am safe.
Okay, it was a lie. But me and the police, we lie to each other—
we bury what they cannot help beneath handfuls of the stuff.
Slush puddles beneath splashes of red and blue.
A man who looks like my father, smells like my father, a man who is
a new constant character of boot polish and bitter tells me I better
not be lying to him. *Lying?* Could be about who I am or
what I am, or which couch I'm sleeping on, or why I left.

(II)

What I am, which couch I'm sleeping on, is the *why*.
To my mother, I am _____ still.
She rings once a year. I do not answer her alcoholic apologism.
We have accepted my absence, meaning we navigate it
with all the grace of two people who do not speak.
I walk my hosts' beagle to piss, his eyes beady,
age-beaten cataract—we stare at the night sky drawn clear
by winter's ragged bite. He thumps his tail thrice and I ask
him the difference between survival and living.
In response, a squad car rolls by, the small-town officer
invisible behind tinted windows except two dull points
revealed by moonlight. Leaving was easy, mom. Clothes.
A fistful of cash. My grandfather's prayer card.

Lone plastic bag receptacle.

(III)
A prayer card and plastic bag birth no comfort within
the police station walls at 2 a.m. I will be liminally useless
the following day. A sacked husk of girl sewn together
by coffee and cigarettes. There is a boy—his jaw meant
for Iowa fistfights, every enemy knuckle white with envy
to caress his granite and Adonis. I dream

        beneath the fluorescent lights of kissing him, lips
tasting of the whiskey sneaked from his dad's oak liqueur cabinet.
My fingers stain nicotine-heat ache. In a decade,
when his jawline grows soft, I hope he is loved.

The officer collapses the distance: heavy boots thud close,
enforce daydream's end.

He says a restraining order is *out of the question.* I do not scream.
The subtext barely concealed.

[Cop father. Cop's daughter.
Don't you get how this works, boy?]

(IV)
Here's how it works:

masquerade laws—
three garments of clothing must match your assigned gender.
Socks and underwear don't count, kid. Do not disguise or obscure
the "biological" self. Queerness as enemy. As fox caught in a trap.
Drag your pelt with you. Raids on clubs. Trans bodies collapsing
in animal cages but pay-it-no-mind sings Ms. Marsha.
Pay-it-no-mind sings the packed bus of kids in handcuffs.

Holy yet hollow is the last time we met. Fingers brushing
the light of a shifting jawline.
Holy are the years we languished hiding from one another
but still knowing. *Still knowing.*

[They're making us illegal again.]

A girl I knew grew up in Kentucky while I grew up in Iowa—
we compared notes on boys who kissed us. Never in public.

(V)
I write love notes to a boy who won't kiss me in public
as lightning bugs scream neon beneath a spiderweb sky.
It will rain, and I will walk the downpour
to a job that pays for a little extra food.
Bread and peanut butter. The trick is to teach the stomach
not to want. Only to consume and imagine full.
A vital lesson for the girl I will one day no longer be. [please]
Maybe she will write poems. Maybe she will not be the same

animal.

The cop car stops
as only cop cars can. *Where are you going?*
asked ad nauseam. *To work. To work.*
I am doing nothing wrong. I am nothing
wrong.

(VI)
Wrong enters in familiar squares of black and white.
The window is open to the breeze, punk-house vinyl
summons the Cranberries singing that same old theme.
Today: graduation. A small-town escape.
The cataract beagle howls at a stalled car's cough.

I paint a lilac-crowned doe in acrylic for
spring has come bearing its switchgrass greens.
I open the door before they can pound—
we all know our places and lines
after the previous "wellness" checks.
Don't cause any trouble today, boy.
We stare. His fists clench. Ms. Marsha was right.
I give an animal's smile and walk into the brush.
They will return.

(VII)
They return, bursting into view as threat
as reminder, as judgment.   To be transgender and homeless
is
an animal thing. We, all of us, walk below,
        along the forest floor

between the smoking pines and toward ourselves
but also away from ourselves. An ever-spiraling wounded stagger
in a country that does not want us.
I drag my pelt wherever I go. My second skin.

Shame. That's what is demanded of me.   I am _____ to them always.

I see it in the eyes.
How dare I be this beast. How dare I want and bark and howl
and be what is made of me.

Within this detested fur,   interrogated nightly,   snarling,

I survive walking lonely Iowa's winter of contempt.

Termi(nation)

KINSALE DRAKE

two gods met & a high rise
        eclipsed the sky   this city unveiled
secret ceremony tucked

beneath urbanscape   in the ads
        real injuns smiled & packed history
into moving trucks   told to gut

the land & call it the chance
        of a lifetime   no need to practice
silly animisms   a city is   nothing

but technoconfusion   chemicals
        churches
in the basements of skyscrapers

they offered replacement god   perfect jobs
        we burn metalwork
in retribution   call it   reclamation:

campfires   in cop cars   imagine
the city filled   with song
        soup can lid jingles   traffic

winking every color
as gods dance   against the metro lines
unfulfilled   as paper injuns

so we body   in cement
in transmission anything
beloved & rugged   our salvation

the final world   is strewn
in cornpollen
so in the cities   in the night

we smear our bodies with the fallout
swear it is just the same

Commandment

KAUAKANILEHUA MĀHOE ADAMS

Thou shalt have no other gods before me.
Exodus 20:3

you arrived in 1820   & told us

our gods had left us

you offered your bibles like gifts
stole our mo'olelo like thieves
shackled us to a word not written for us
who knew the divine did not reign unseen
but lived within

all the stars   skies   mountains   & seas
within the moon & all her moods   the sun & all his jealousy
every drop of rain
every seed to sprout   every flower on the brink of bloom
every tree hung heavy with fruit
every fish   every bird
every stacked stone   every purling stream
in the ali'i & the people
in my grandfather & his children
in my heart & my brother's & sister's too

we are the children of the sky & the stars

woven together by what you thought you could take
your make-believe
                                    our truth
that our gods could never leave us
            when they've always lived within us

D DAVIS 2025

1972

HANNAH V. SAWYERR

The year is 2022.
I sit in front of my 2022 Roku TV
when Bree hits my DMs on 2022 Twitter,
with an article that rolls time back fifty years:

**"Supreme Court overturns Roe v. Wade,
ending right to abortion upheld for decades"**

"Look at this shit"   she sends in a text attached
& we facetime on our 2022 iPhones

confusion on face & laced in tone   we scroll
& over the loudest (<1973) silence   we joke:

The Supreme Court wants babies outta us
          more than our mamas do!

we laugh   in that way we do
when a joke is only funny   because aint shit funny

because today in the year 2022
six votes overturned a fifty-year ruling
regarding wombs which five of the voters
do not have

today   in the year 2022
six votes decided our agency is collateral damage
for a country's control

today   in the year 2022
it's easier to laugh than admit our body's choice
has been challenged today
& long before 1973:

over one hundred years ago
when abortion was criminalized in all US states

Over fifty years ago
when Dr. Jane Hodgson was convicted
for providing a patient with an abortion

less than one year ago
when over one hundred abortion restrictions were enacted—
the most the country has seen in a single year

& just five minutes ago
when Bree hit my phone with an article like: *look at this shit.*

That night I dream of a day
when my body knows more peace than protest

when bodies and autonomy hold more value
in our country than religion and guns

when choice feels more guarantee
& less luxury

My body—today in 2022 & every day
after will be a home for all the fight
& grit & gall we have gained in the face of anyone
who challenges choice in the name
of a God who they pretend to be, do not know
& can only dream of being.

Elegy for Slavery: Middle Passage to Hip-Hop

RONALD GREER

In 1619 when the slave ship *White Lion* roared over the tides of the
Atlantic our future swayed in the bowels,
chained like King Kong. All we wanted was home.

Dear Slavery, did you manifest destiny when you floated a million
Black bodies through the Middle Passage singing kumbaya?

Did you care that Black bodies crave the African sun, never needed
ocean waves and shackles, cholera, and to be stacked
like slabs of ribs in a slow cooker? We lost everything.

Then we lost more in the day break to day break
bend back bloody-hand cotton-picking labor.

What more motivation does one need than a shackled body
picking cotton?

The story goes "If I was a slave I would have . . ."

Done what? Been a slave.

Dear Chattel Slavery, did you manifest destiny when you kidnapped
and raped a nation to
convert them to cotton pickers?

When we say we got it out the mud. It's literal.
Our ancestors rose themselves out of the mud

soldiered rivers by the light of the North Star.

Our ancestors stuck bare feet into muddy swamps dragging a baby
they didn't birth so its life was worth more than "pick a bale of cotton."
Cotton. It's always a cotton picker that triggers me. But

don't forget the castrations
tar and feathers
strange fruit dangling,
Bill of Rights restricted,
hog maws, chittlin chewing,
bloody finger, cotton picking, swamp running,
minstrel show, birth of a nation.

When you do.
There is no growth in reflection.
There is nothing to prevail.

Our culture was stripped from us, but from restriction, conviction was born
determined to be felt we stomped our feet into the ground
and caused earthquakes
determined to be heard we sang high notes to the heavens
and spit sugar-laced lyrics
determined to be seen we turned our rags into bright suits,
big hats, and bling.

Our dream was deferred
but we keep dreaming because yesterday is blood trauma
and our culture tells us that we will prevail. Some

Go Tell It on the Mountain, or wanna know What's Going On?
others have a 7 Day Theory. Some Party and Bull,
or know when the Drill about come,
others is twerking on them headlights at red light. And I love it.

My mother's music spoke of love and revolution.
My music speaks of love and revolution.
If you listen close enough, all music speaks of love and revolution

and tragedy.

We took the lash of bull whips and turned them into new whips,
took the shackles and manacles and turned them
into diamond encrusted bracelets,
chain thicker than any iron neck fixture affixed to the necks of a coffle.

Everything is the blues and we smother the world with it no matter
the beat.

The beat. Like thirty lashes to a king chained to a tree.

Our culture was beat from us.
Our heritage was beat from us.
When whips tried to beat the hope from us.

We beat our marks
on America with murals
over murder colored walls.
Our quick loose tongues
forced suburbanites to confess their love.
Pants saggin. Chain swangin.
They don't even know
what they imitate are thugs.
Thugs imitate radicals.
Radicals imitate abolitionists,
and abolitionists
were just hopeful slaves
who hummed the freedom
of hip-hop over bales of cotton.

DDAVIS

say it with your whole black mouth

DANEZ SMITH

say it with your whole black mouth: i am innocent.
& if you are not innocent, say this: i am worthy

of forgiveness, of breath after breath.
i tell you this: i let blue eyes dress me in guilt

walked around stores convinced the very skin
of my palm was stolen. what good has it brought?

days filled flinching thinking the sirens
were reaching for me. & when the sirens were mine

did i not make peace with God?
so many white people are alive

because we know how to control ourselves.
how many times have we died on a whim

wielded like gallows in their sun-shy hands?
here, standing in my own body, i say: next time

they murder us for the crime of their imaginations
i don't know what i'll do.

i did not come to preach of peace
for that's not the hunted's duty.

i came here to say what i can't say
without my name being added to a list

what my mother fears i will say
what she wishes to say herself

i came here to say

The Lord is American

W. J. LOFTON

The world undresses
its wounds. It wounds. This Father—
His memory, torn
clouds: forgetful weather.
God's goodness licks
bowls bone-clean. Our fingers
twist crumbs from air.
We are hungry children
abandoned by our country
for bombs. For Rockets' Red glare. How
could we ever be patriots?
My father is my flag.
The national anthem is
every word, every single word
my mother could not whisper—
could not say,
could not say:

her father colonized her.
Made her mother nasty with jealousy.
Could not say: she can't stay
In this world of touching.
It maims.
It elects evil.
It is two gendered.
It kneels on Sunday.
The Lord is
American &
aims His rifle
at us, His children
once beggars
rise into guerrillas.

A Year Since We Took the City

TAIWANA SHAMBLEY

In Saint Paul's North End neighborhood lived two sisters who spent their after preschool hours training on rooftops cosplaying as their favorite Black mythology characters. They swung bo staffs, splitting all the air in their area in half and moving them like tides from the Great Lakes, strikes they saw in last night's pilot episode of *Daughters of Oya*. The sisters were twins and close, but didn't know if they wanted to be the first; the younger accented her gi with a Raphael red, a strip here and a patch there, where the older opted for a headband with the Leaf symbol scratched out. In the summers, they joined their mother Jaslene in Denver to practice on the most comfortable mid-sized mountain they could find, creating thrusts and arcs with new history. A year before they were born, their mother Taiwana messed around and built an autonomous neighborhood with her cousins. *White nationalists killed thirteen babies,* the girls remembered hearing Big Cousin's voice on the screen, courtesy of the free New State commercials. The girls were about to mute it had not a photo of their mom claimed the screen. *White nationalists killed thirteen babies cause they were brown so a group calling themselves the Thirteen Triggers told them to remove their politicians and police from Saint Paul or they're offering thirteen of 'em.* One night, after the girls went to sleep, Taiwana hears knocks on her front door like a car crash, car crashes, then three, so already she knows who it is.

She opens it and her little cousin pushes through her living room and makes her way to the kitchen. She pokes her head around in the fridge then faces Taiwana, leaning against the wall, body tilting at an angle so clean and straight it's geometry. Her cousin brushes the ends of her jean jacket, runs her fingers through the thick of her Malaysian Body Wave styled hair dyed purple at the ends, holds her arms across her chest and complains that all Taiwana drinks is filtered water, who then shakes her head and lets a chuckle go. The cousin says,

—So whats been up with you? You know KK and I bout to go on patrol. Its only been a year since we took the city.

—I *just* put the kids to sleep.

The cousin steps into the living room, looks around, and fiddles with whatever's on the TV stand.

—And, what, you forget to answer your phone?

—My fault, Cuz. I've just been busy.

Blue Doritos bags. Casamigos bottles tumbling out the recycling. Dried out mangos.

—Too busy takin care of my little cousins, or too busy broodin round in this house? It looks sad in here, Cuz.

—Is there something you wanted?

—I just think its funny cause you got a babysitter. Everybody, cause of what we did, has childcare. Im tryna figure out whats really up.

—It's nothin.
—Its somethin.

—I'm good.

—Okay.

They hear the 3A pass by and stop.

—**Its good seein you.**

The cousin makes her way to the door, struggling with the lock. Then,

—**Cuz. I know why we did what we did. If we build it here, then we have to defend it. And if we don't defend it, then every brown kid lives a half-life. But this ain't even our land for real. How are the kids going to look at us?**

—**Damn . . . You sound just like her.**

The cousin plops down next to Taiwana on the couch, closing the space between them so their knees just about touch. The 3A closes its doors and hums as it drives away. Then they hear one, two yells they can't quite make out.

—**You know you the one who wanted to do the blockade, right? Matter or fact, remember *Beloved?***

—**I put you on to *Beloved*.**

—**You wouldnt tell Sethe she shouldve handed her kids back to slavery.**

—**I'm not saying that.**

—**Then what you sayin?**

—**I just feel like you liked it too much.**

The cousin was standing now.

—**Is that what you think? Im out here slicin throats? Me and your sister out here bombin babies?**

—**You're going to wake my kids up.**

—**And you always weaponizin my little cousins! They need to hear this.**

—**Why?**

-**Cause one day they might need to take us down!**

Silence. There's a tree in the front yard. The wind weighs down a branch, and they hear it brush against a window. Then,

—**You must be tryna detox or sum huh? Is that what all them lemons for?**

—**You must be about to leave.**

She shuts the door after her cousin, locks the bottom, then the top, and steps into the kitchen. She drinks the water, slowly, like a lady, enjoying the cold in her throat and belly. The girls gently pull their ears away from the bedroom door, just before the knob turns and it begins to push open.

Serve and Protect

KEKLA MAGOON

patrolling the community while armed
to protect the people
they talk the talk
we walk the walk

clothe the poor and feed the hungry
treat a stranger as your brother
they talk the talk
we walk the walk

we hold these truths to be self-evident
all power to the people
they talk the talk
we walk the walk

D DAVIS 2025

After Abolition

KYLE CARRERO LOPEZ

Prisons and cops survive only in tales for the young
like twin Atlantises or two drowned boogeymen.
A cop's as harmless a Halloween getup as any
monster, while a prisoner costume's as taboo as a slave one
now that schools teach what makes them kin.
A prison is the far-off past of a structure
turned free housing, each cell wall knocked to sandcastle
ruin, halls reshaped and re-dyed in green paints,
former floor plans carved out like shores
into spacious homes, laundry and A/C a given in each.
Though prisons and cops won't be found anywhere,
our youths still learn of them, and they know what they mean,
how they look, how they function, what it will take to stop them
if they return with new names.

my recipe for freedom OR if you see me in my backyard singing, mind yo' business

MARIAMA J. LOCKINGTON

the sun fraying the edges
        of a cold morning
my dog, Henry, in the yard
making circles in the frosted grass

a song in my throat
        primal & round
begging to be sung
        no matter the neighbors
        no matter the sleep
        still ringing all through my bones

how to explain   my container of a body
        rendered dumb under
a sky so blue it aches & speaks to me
        like a distant mother

        how to explain   that all the sweetness
        in the world
        cannot dull the grief of having
                made it   this far
                when so many of us die
                before we know
                the shape of our own names

Black lilies
        wilted & squashed
        under some dirty boot
        as if we were meant
        to live only   as buried things

I look at my little yard:
the decayed garden beds
the stump of a dead honeysuckle
        littered with creeping charlie
        robins fighting for nest territory

        squirrels tightroping the fence

        & despite the chaos
        the violent shadows
of collective memory
hazing my vision
        I delight in what thorns
        I have dug out of my skin

        I focus on what love scuttles
        the property
& refuses to
        stay still

I stand in my yard
like one of the tall pin oaks
rooted, & yes—also dying
& somewhere between the seed of my shame
& the bud of my power

my voice comes
rushing
I raise my throat
to the daylight
I mess through a guttural wail
my mouth blooming
green symphonies

I cannot stay quiet
I cannot stay hidden

I am so hungry
all my songs   full of honey
and rapture

D DAVIS 2025

I'm Not Bear Clan, But

HALEE KIRKWOOD

so many of my friends are.

In their heartsongs, they carry ancestors
who used to be our community protectors,

walking the village edge and searching
as much for plant medicine as they did

for danger. I thought of them
the week George Floyd was murdered.

The day I found the blackberry bush
heavy with ripe and dripping fruit.

The blackberry bush twisting
through the diamond-shaped gaps

in the flimsy fence separating us
from the interstate,

the brambles we could see
the national guard gathering through.

Fruit dropped everywhere
that spring, crushed and staining

both the sidewalk and the boot.
Unnamed, ungathered, uneaten.

Bear clan is the most populous clan,
and in this way the responsibility

to protect and heal
is everyone's business. As in:

Miskwaabiimizh and Miskomin
Willow bark and raspberry leaf

Giizhik and Ode'imin and Giizisobagoons
Cedar and strawberry and purple coneflower

as in there are as many ways
to protect your community as there are

tender green roots at your feet.
I dream your ancestors handing mine—

mikinaak, that gentle turtle—
a bundle of sweet medicines,

our hands softly touching.
I dream our ancestors fierce

with the strength and love
of a mother bear and then I dream

ourselves like that,
the good ancestors we must become.

After they left

MICHAEL KLEBER-DIGGS

we policed ourselves, restored our spirits
in quiet tasks until the earth ran red
with iron and sweat. We called old seeds
from the cavernous cold to rejoin them
with the heartsick soil, then tended our crops by hand.
Every day everyone

bent down on knees to pull the weeds away.
Pests took their part but left plenty.
Each harvest, the village gathered together.
To each a share. For all it had suffered

our body stayed whole. Trauma dissipated.
Where our wounds were acute, we applied more balm,
calling our injured closer in, as we sang to them
and gave them more fruit.

Additional Poem Notes

CAROLYN HOLBROOK

I wrote "Speaking in the Silence" after experiencing Miré Regulus's installation, *The Other Side House*, an instillation that was designed to ask, "What is on the other side of grief?"

While listening to John Coltrane in that wonderfully healing space, I thought about my siblings and parents, my son, and other ancestors who have passed on. But I found myself focusing on my three siblings who I lost over a period of ten years, before any of us reached middle age.

As the last surviving sibling, I have often questioned why I am the one who has been allowed to survive into elderhood. The only reason I can think of is that I must still have work to do before I leave the planet.

The losses of my siblings coupled with the loss of my parents and now my son have gifted me with a profound desire to honor the power of their love, their stories, and their memories, and to keep trying to pass that love on to future generations in whatever ways I can.

SUN YUNG SHIN

This poem is about a display case at the Smith & Wesson Gallery of Firearms History at the Springfield Museums in Massachusetts. I have been researching the history of firearms in the United States, our gun culture, and the US's role as the world's largest arms dealer. It is a "loose sonnet" that I chose in order to bring some formal containment to this subject, like a museum vitrine. My work often explores the ways language is used to justify domination and desecration, and how racial capitalism demands our dissociation from everything good. This poem explores the fetishization of iconic tools of American law enforcement; nature (always) and ordinary human beings (always) are conscripted into committing the ruling class's atrocities and bottomless sadism. The italics are a Greek chorus; we are collectively complicit in our society's delusions of heroism. The poem was written within a year of my 2022 visit to the gallery.

D. R. BERNSTROM

"Last Words" laments the death of Oscar Grant at Fruitvale Station. It is a modern elegy, which is a poetic form that explores loss, sorrow, and consolation through vivid imagery. Reflecting Oscar's aspiration to be a pastor and his religious upbringing, the poem evokes the musicality of a Black preacher's voice, echoing the cadences that might have been heard at his funeral. While classical elegies adhere to metrical patterns, I intentionally twist or break patterns to convey a sense of injustice and wrongness in an effort to contrast the Black experience with the rigidity of current police practices. The fractured meter deliberately creates discomfort in the reader. (We should not be comfortable.) This deliberate awkwardness and lack of resolution underscore the poem's themes of injustice, brokenness, and irreparable harm.

LAURA RUBY

I've been grappling with my father's years as a cop for a long time, but this poem is my first attempt in print. I chose to write a cento, a form that uses language gathered from other poems—or, in this case, newspapers—because I wanted to understand how my ideas of policing came not just from my father but also from the media and the culture in which we live, and how he, as an olive-skinned Jewish man, was occasionally targeted by members of his own profession. I wish I'd asked more questions when he was alive.

KAO KALIA YANG

This is a biographical poem. Yia died in Stillwater, Minnesota, in the Saint Croix River. Years later, my father took my sister and me to the place where Yia died so we could see it. We were stopped by police. The officer said Dad was going over the limit. He was not. In court, he had to pay the ticket anyway because we had no proof and Dad's English was limited. Yia had been a good English speaker and translated for Dad many times in the past.

JASON REYNOLDS

"This Has Always Been Our Active Shooter Drill" is a poem that comments on the dissonance between the active shooter drills children all over America are forced to carry out in the event of a school shooter and the often futile drill that black parents execute with their children (even once they become adults) to hopefully protect them from abusive police officers who identify them as targets and not as people.

ARI TISON

I've passed 38th and Chicago thousands of times. I guess that's the part about home being home, it just *is*. Home to all sorts of humanness, beauty, and complication, like any place. I've lived in rural areas and cities, visited nearly every state, and I'm both stunned by reality of others' daily lives, but also by the same gambit of need manifested in all sorts of ways. Like many others in this world, I wasn't lacking in suffering in my childhood and young adulthood.

The act of prayer has been a steadfast practice of mine. I hadn't realized that horror could take even my words to God away. They'd never left me before. The murder of George Floyd was horrific. And during the time many spoke for our city, I had to mourn so deeply that my voice had to be quiet. And when the time was right, it was my community who invited my voice back.

PADMA VENKATRAMAN

I left India on my own at the age of nineteen. When I was pulled over by a policeman in a rural part of southern Virginia one night, I had no idea of what to expect. For a while, until I shared it with friends, I had no reference, no context, no idea of the danger of the situation. Even now, the memory feels as surreal as it is frightening. Although my poem was written decades after the incident, I still see the officer's fingers in my nightmares.

TAE KELLER

In 2024, there were over ten thousand unsheltered people living on the streets of Seattle. Rather than implementing proven solutions like Housing First initiatives, the city has enacted thousands of "sweeps," in which police sweep through neighborhoods, trashing unhoused residents' tents, documents, and other belongings, and forcing them to move elsewhere. The city spends $30 million a year on these sweeps, only to see increases in overdoses, hospitalizations, and deaths. All the while, the number of people living on the streets has risen.

Yet, houselessness is not an unsolvable problem. Other cities and countries have addressed it effectively. We have the resources—now we must use those resources not for *punishment* but for protection and support, for all of us, for the collective good.

Read more about the sweeps at https://www.realchangenews.org/news/2024/06/05/sweeps-tripled-2023.

OLLIE SCHMINKEY

A contrapuntal is a form poem that is intended to be read as three combined poems: the left column creates one poem, the right column creates another, and a third poem is created when the two columns are read across together. The "magic" of a contrapuntal is when meaning is shifted or created in that third reading. I chose this form because it allowed me to capture the way that joy transforms into fear through regressive and harmful policies.

This poem was written in response to an overwhelming increase in anti-trans legislation introduced and passed in 2023 across the United States (at least five hundred anti-trans bills were introduced nationwide, over half impacting trans youth). These bills targeted transgender people's access to health care, education, sports, and bathrooms, and they represent a growing nationwide attack on the rights of trans people.

To find out more about anti-trans bills, go to translegislation.com/learn.

K. A. HOLT

"Uvalde Villain-elle" was written after the January 2024 release of the United States Justice Department's report on the law enforcement response to the horrific school shooting at Robb Elementary School in Uvalde, Texas. The number of law enforcement agencies mentioned in this poem, as well as the number of law enforcement personnel present at the scene, the timing of the law enforcement response that day, and the number of lives lost, all come directly from the numbers reported in the Justice Department's Critical Incident Review.

As far as structuring the poem, there was really only one choice to be made: the complex-to-conceive, but precise-to-read, traditional villanelle.

"Uvalde Villain-elle" is dedicated to Nevaeh, Jackie, Makenna, Jose, Ellie, Irma, Uziyah, Amerie Jo, Xavier, Jayce, Tess, Maranda, Eva, Alithia, Annabell, Maite, Lexi, Layla, Jalilah, Eliahna, and Rojelio.

DOUGLAS KEARNEY

"Designed for Off the Chain" is from a series of poems called *Dark Matter Armory Flex*. Each poem is a digital collage combining a component of Gothic armor with a Black diasporic musical feature. I chose collage because I love sample-based musical production. This poem is a call-and-response gorget. Call-and-response is a feature of many Black oral/musical traditions (from church to concerts to protests); a gorget protects the wearer's neck. "Designed for Off the Chain" specifically alludes to events in May 2020, when murderer Derek Chauvin, who was a Minneapolis police officer at the time, killed George Floyd by kneeling on his neck, asphyxiating him. However, a gorget would help guard against any number of brutal acts involving the victim's neck and throat. You can find the rest of the series—and other visual poems—in the book *I Imagine I Been Science Fiction Always*.

ALICE PAIGE

"Masquerade laws" refer to a collection of city ordinances and state laws across America throughout the eighteenth and nineteenth centuries that banned cross-dressing. Some of these regulations required individuals to wear at least three garments of clothing that match their assigned gender at birth. Socks and underwear often did not count toward this three-garment requirement.

"Ms. Marsha" is another moniker for Marsha P. Johnson, a transgender activist and icon in New York in the 1960s and '70s. A phrase she often employed when faced with the question of gender was "Pay it no mind."

KINSALE DRAKE

The title "Termi(nation)" refers to the Termination Era & relocation policies of the 1950s–1960s, which formally began with House Concurrent Resolution 108: "All of the Indian tribes and the individual members thereof located within the States of California, Florida, New York, and Texas, should be freed from Federal supervision and control and all disabilities and limitations specifically applicable to Indians." Over one hundred tribes were terminated from federal assistance and the Bureau of Indian Affairs (BIA) established multiple field relocation offices to relocate Native peoples to cities and forcibly assimilate them. Today, about 70 percent of Native peoples live in urban areas, according to the Urban Indian Health Institute.

KAUAKANILEHUA MĀHOE ADAMS

In 1820 Calvinist missionaries arrived in Hawai'i to evangelize the Kānaka Maoli (Native Hawaiians). The missionaries' presence ultimately paved the way to the overthrow of the Hawaiian government and the United States' continued illegal occupation of the Hawaiian kingdom.

DANEZ SMITH

In the summer of 2017, I was roommates at the VONA writers' retreat with Junot Díaz, Marjorie Liu, and David Mura in the best summer-camp dream a writer could ask for. I don't remember who had been murdered, or even if someone had, but one night David and I got to talking about race, guilt, anger, action, and our hometowns of Minneapolis and Saint Paul. I left that conversation too raw to go to bed, too vulnerable to walk it off, so this poem came out of me. I don't even know if it's a poem to be real. It's a feeling? A declaration? Maybe one stop short of a declaration. It's something I had to write to be able to move around the world, to know that my experience in America, in my body, in my black, hunted, endangered, beautiful, worthy body is as (blank) as it seems to be. And the poem is the one safe place I feel I can put these possibly violent impulses without doing (justified) damage.

W. J. LOFTON

I rarely felt safe as a child. The closest I've felt to safety was hanging with my cousins or being by my older sisters' side[s]. Even then, I felt danger huffing about, stalking me. As a child whose parents suffered premature deaths due to America's inadequate health care and mental health systems, I'm often thinking about children and how they are wrestled down by adult failures. The world's cruelty shows itself to children through adults, even before they learn words like war, ceasefire and, later, genocide. I believe we owe children a world that loves them, and we must struggle for it at any cost.

KEKLA MAGOON

In the 1960s, the Black Panther Party responded to the issue of police brutality in Black communities by carrying guns of their own and policing the police. They later expanded this neighborhood self-defense effort by providing food, clothing, and advocacy, creating survival programs to address the people's most urgent needs. Further, they challenged the United States to truly become a nation "of the people, by the people, and for the people," suggesting ways to return power to citizens who had long been disenfranchised and oppressed by capitalism and systemic racism. "Serve and protect" is a motto often used by police departments, but the three stanzas in this poem ask, What does it really mean to serve and to protect?

MARIAMA J. LOCKINGTON

This poem was inspired by a prompt from my POC women and femmes writing group. We were asked to write a recipe for freedom—to explore when and how we feel most free. I've always been a secret singer—belting out in dark karaoke bars, jamming in my house, and sometimes writing my own lyrics. I became a first-time homeowner in 2021, and every time I take my dogs out back, I feel a tremendous sense of gratitude and awe that I get to call this place home. As an adopted person, a queer person, and a person who has moved around a lot in life, the concept of home has always been tricky. This poem is a manifestation of the joy, freedom, and grief I feel all at once at having made it to this moment, at having carved out a little place of belonging.

HALEE KIRKWOOD

This poem had been brewing inside me since George Floyd's murder in 2020. It was a surreal, scary time for everyone in the Twin Cities, which was contrasted with a spring explosion of plants, blackberries seemingly everywhere I looked in the Stevens Square neighborhood, National Guard soldiers posted on our street corners, and our community centers, grocery stores, and pharmacies destroyed by fires. On Franklin Avenue, I was inspired by local Native community members taking community safety into their own hands during a time that so many of us felt spitefully abandoned by the MPD. They made me think of the Bear clan, who are largely considered the warrior clan in Anishinaabe social structures. Too often, warriorhood is only associated with the perceived necessity of physical force, but I want to imagine a world where warriorhood means the bravery to be kind in a world that all too often honors cruelty, a world where warriorhood is synonymous with healing.

MICHAEL KLEBER-DIGGS

"After they left," was written in 2016 while I participated in a writing fellowship with ten other Black writers. We spent a year sharing work and ideas with one another under the guidance of two amazing mentors, the poets Mary Moore Easter and Danez Smith.

I often write about the world I inhabit—what makes it horrifying and what makes it beautiful. And at the time, I was writing a lot about loss, both the loss of my father, who died when I was young, and the loss of Black American lives to police violence.

One of my friends from the program, Erin Sharkey, encouraged me to write a poem imagining a future without policing. Her prompt opened a world of possibilities for me. I began to imagine the kind of world I'd like to live in. "After they left," reminds me that while documenting is important, so is dreaming.

About the Poets

Kauakanilehua Māhoe Adams is a mixed Native Hawaiian author and poet with an MFA in writing for young people from Vermont College of Fine Arts. She was a finalist for the 2025 Steve Kowit Poetry Prize and her debut novel, *An Expanse of Blue*, came out in 2026.

D. R. Bernstrom is an award-winning author of seven picture books. His joyful books, including the Minnesota Book Award–winner *Big Papa and the Time Machine*, have received national recognition and critical acclaim. He teaches literature and writing at Minnesota West Community & Technical College.

Fong Li Blessing is an artist and storyteller based in Saint Paul, Minnesota. He is a celebrated poet, with publications through the Minnesota Prison Writing Workshop and Asian American Writers' Workshop, a beloved painter, and a published photographer.

Ty Chapman is an award-winning author and poet based in Minnesota. He is the author of many children's books as well as the poetry collection *Tartarus*. He has published poems through the Academy of American Poets, *Water~Stone Review*, and more.

Kinsale Drake (Diné) is a winner of the National Poetry Series for her debut poetry collection *The Sky Was Once a Dark Blanket*, also named a Southwest Book of the Year. A two-time winner of the Academy of American Poets University Prize and former National Student Poet, her work has appeared in *Poetry*, Poets.org, *Best New Poets*, and elsewhere. She directs programming for NDN Girls Book Club and lives and teaches in Nashville, Tennessee, as a graduate fellow at Vanderbilt University.

Margarita Engle is the Cuban-American author of many verse novels, which have received Pura Belpré honors and medals, Walter Honors, Américas Awards, a Jane Addams Award, a PEN Center USA Award, and the NSK Neustadt Prize. Engle served as the national 2017–2019 Young People's Poet Laureate. Her most recent verse novel is *Island Creatures*.

Amanda Gorman is the youngest Presidential inaugural poet in US history. She is a committed advocate for the environment, racial equality, and gender justice. The special edition of her inaugural poem, "The Hill We Climb," was published in March 2021. Later that year, her debut picture book, *Change Sings*, and her poetry collection, *Call Us What We Carry*, were released, each debuting at #1 on *New York Times*, *USA Today*, and *Wall Street Journal* bestseller lists. In 2023, her second picture book, *Something Someday*, released as a bestseller, and *Call Us What We Carry* was nominated for a Grammy Award for Best Spoken Word Poetry Album. In 2025, Amanda was named a UNICEF Ambassador.

A poet by nature and a daydreamer by necessity, **Ronald Greer** is from Detriot, Michigan. He's published in *A Darker Wilderness: Black Nature Writing from Soil to Stars* and is an editor of *American Precariat: Parables of Exclusion*. He is a member of Minnesota Prison Writers Workshop.

New York Times best-selling author **Nikki Grimes**, a Black Authors Hall of Fame inductee, is a recipient of the Virginia Hamilton Lifetime Achievement Award, ALAN Award, Children's Literature Legacy Medal, NCTE Award for Excellence in Poetry, and the Coretta Scott King Award. *Ordinary Hazards*, her banned memoir, received both Printz and Sibert Honors.

Carolyn Holbrook's memoir, *Tell Me Your Names and I Will Testify*, won a Minnesota Book Award in 2021. She is coeditor with David Mura of *We Are Meant to Rise: Voices for Justice from Minneapolis to the World* and is the founder and director of More Than a Single Story (morethanasinglestory.com). She is the 2025 McKnight Distinguished Artist.

K. A. Holt is the author of more than fifteen books for young readers, including the award-winning middle grade novels-in-verse *House Arrest*, *Redwood and Ponytail*, and the Kids Under the Stairs series. She is a founding member of the public radio phenomenon, Typewriter Rodeo, a globetrotting, truth-bearing troupe of spontaneous poets based in Austin, Texas.

Douglas Kearney has published nine books ranging from poetry to essays. In 2023, *Optic Subwoof*, a collection of his Bagley Wright lectures, won the Poetry Foundation's Pegasus Award for Poetry Criticism and the CLMP Firecracker Award for Creative Nonfiction. His seventh, *Sho*, is a Griffin Poetry Prize and Minnesota Book Award winner and a National Book Award, Pen America, and Kingsley Tufts Award finalist.

Tae Keller is the Newbery Award–winning and #1 *New York Times* best-selling author of *When You Trap a Tiger* and *The Science of Breakable Things*. Born and raised in Hawai'i, she now lives in Seattle with her husband, dog, and a multitude of books. When she's not writing, she teaches at Hamline University in their writing for children and young adults master's program.

Erin Entrada Kelly is a two-time Newbery Medalist and National Book Award Finalist whose work has been translated into more than a dozen languages. She is a *New York Times* best-selling author and teaches in the writing for children and young adults master's program at Hamline University. She has a bachelor's degree in liberal arts from McNeese University, an MFA in fiction from Rosemont College, and an honorary doctorate of fine arts from Moore College of Art and Design. She lives in Delaware.

Halee Kirkwood is a poet, teaching artist, and bookseller living in Minneapolis, Minnesota. Their debut poetry book, *To Think of a Match*, is forthcoming in 2027. Kirkwood is the winner of the 2022 James Welch Prize, published with *Poetry Northwest*. They have had work published in *Poetry*, *Prairie Schooner*, *Gulf Coast*, *Water~Stone Review*, Poem-a-Day, and elsewhere.

Michael Kleber-Diggs is a poet, essayist, literary critic, and arts educator. He is the author of *My Weight in Water: Notes of a Fat Black Swimmer*, a memoir about his complicated relationship with lap swimming. His debut poetry collection, *Worldly Things*, won the 2021 Max Ritvo Poetry Prize.

Ada Limón is the author of seven books of poetry, including *The Hurting Kind*, which was a finalist for the Griffin Prize; *The Carrying*, which won the National Books Critics Circle Award and was a finalist for the PEN/Jean Stein Book Award; and *Bright Dead Things*, which was named a finalist for the National Book Award, the National Book Critics Circle Award, and the Kingsley Tufts Award. She is the author of two picture books, and she served as the 24th Poet Laureate of the United States.

Mariama J. Lockington is an adoptee, educator, and an award-winning author of books for teens and tweens. She holds a M.Ed from Lesley University and an MFA in poetry from San Francisco State University. She calls many places home but currently lives in Kentucky with her wife, her sausage dogs, and an abundance of plants.

W. J. Lofton is a Black Queer Southern poet and multimodal artist. He is the author of *boy maybe* and *A Garden for Black Boys Between the Stages of Soil and Stardust*. Lofton's constant concern is liberation and its lived manifestations—the personal, political, and collective. He lives in Atlanta, Georgia.

Kyle Carrero Lopez is the author of *Party Line*. A Cave Canem fellow, he serves as editor for the *Poetry Project Newsletter*. His poetry is published in *The Yale Review, The Nation, Poetry, The New Republic*, and elsewhere.

Kekla Magoon writes novels and nonfiction books for children and teens, often on themes of identity, community, empowerment, and social justice. Acclaimed titles include *The Season of Styx Malone, The Rock and the River, How It Went Down*, and *Revolution in Our Time: The Black Panther Party's Promise to the People*.

Kyle Tran Myhre is a poet and activist based in Minneapolis, Minnesota. He's performed at the United Nations, contributed to a Grammy-winning album, been a member of two National Poetry Slam championship teams, and visited countless colleges, conferences, and festivals, using spoken word and storytelling as doorways into critical dialogue.

Alice Paige is an anti-fascist educator at Hamline University and a former homeless queer youth. Her work centers on the transformative power of queer joy, the futures we have yet to imagine, and the years we have traversed to reach one another.

Junauda Petrus is a creative activist, writer, playwright, and multi-dimensional performance artist who was born on Dakota land, West-Indian descended, and African-sourced. Her work centers on Black wildness, futurism, ancestral healing, sweetness, spectacle, and shimmer. She is the author of *The Stars and the Blackness Between Them*, a 2020 Coretta Scott King Book Award author honor title.

Bao Phi is a Vietnamese American spoken word artist, poet, children's book writer, and essayist whose work has been widely published in individual volumes as well as anthologies, including *Thousand Star Hotel, A Different Pond, Octavia's Brood: Science Fiction Stories from Social Justice Movements*, and *A Good Time for the Truth: Race in Minnesota*. He is a community member, a refugee, and a father.

Jason Reynolds is a #1 *New York Times* best-selling author of many award-winning books, including *Look Both Ways: A Tale Told in Ten Blocks, All American Boys* (with Brendan Kiely), *Long Way Down*, and others. Reynolds was a recipient of a Newbery Honor, a Printz Honor, an NAACP Image Award, and multiple Coretta Scott King honors. Reynolds was also the 2020–2022 National Ambassador for Young People's Literature.

Karuna Riazi is a YA and middle grade author, educator, and diversity advocate. She is the author of *The Gauntlet* and its companion *The Battle*. Her contributions may also be found in anthologies such as *Here We Are: Feminism for the Real World, How I Resist: Activism and Hope for the Next Generation*, and *Unbroken: 13 Stories Starring Disabled Teens*.

A two-time National Book Award Finalist, **Laura Ruby** writes fiction and poetry for adults, teens, and children. She is the author of the Printz Medal–winning novel *Bone Gap*, as well as *Thirteen Doorways, Wolves Behind Them All*. Her poetry has appeared or is forthcoming in *Diode, Sugar House Review, Fantasy Magazine, Poetry South, The Dallas Review, The Nassau Review, Passengers Journal, Prism Review*, and *Clackamas Literary Review*.

Aida Salazar is an award-winning author, translator, and arts activist. Her critically acclaimed verse novels and picture books have received over twenty-five awards including a Caldecott Honor, a Pura Belpré Honor, an Américas Award, a Tomás Rivera Book Award, a NSK Neustadt Finalist, and International Latino Book Awards, among other distinctions.

Hannah V. Sawyerr is an award-winning poet and young adult novelist. Her spoken word has been featured on the BBC's *World Have Your Say* program as well as the National Education Association's "Do You Hear Us?" campaign. Her written word has been included in *Essence* and *xoNecole*. Her novels include 2024 Morris Award finalist and Walter Award honor *All the Fighting Parts* and National Book Award longlisted title *Truth Is*.

Ollie Schminkey has spent over a decade coaching, teaching classes, and running workshops for poets. They've performed poems in twenty-one states, with work appearing in Poets.org, *Frontier Poetry*, and more. They are the author of two full-length collections: *Dead Dad Jokes* and *Where I Dry the Flowers*.

A Black trans woman with disabilities, **Taiwana Shambley** is a speculative fiction writer and award-winning teaching artist from the North End neighborhood of Saint Paul, Minnesota.

Sun Yung Shin is an award-winning multi-genre author of thirteen books. Her most recent picture book is *Revolutions Are Made of Love: The Story of James Boggs and Grace Lee Boggs*; her latest book for adults is *Heart Eater: A Memoir of Immigration, Belonging, and How We Find Ourselves in Language*. Born in Korea, Shin lives in Minneapolis, Minnesota, on Dakota land.

Danez Smith was born in Saint Paul, Minnesota. They are the author of *Bluff*; *Don't Call Us Dead*, a finalist for the National Book Award; and *[insert] Boy*, winner of the Lambda Literary Award and the Kate Tufts Discovery Award.

Ari Tison (Bribri) is a poet and the author of *Together We See* and hybrid poetry and prose novel *Saints of the Household*, which won the Walter Dean Myers Award and the Pura Belpré Award and was a finalist for the William C. Morris Award. Her poetry has been published in various literary journals including *Yellow Medicine Review* and *Poetry*.

Padma Venkatraman's poetry has been published in *Poetry* and nominated for the Pushcart Prize. She is the founder of www.diverseverse.org and the author of five novels including *The Bridge Home* (Global Read Aloud and Walter Dean Myers Award winner) and *A Time to Dance* (the first South Asian novel-in-verse in English for young people).

Jasmine Warga is the #1 *New York Times* best-selling and award-winning author of many books for young readers, including *A Rover's Story*, *Other Words for Home*, and *The Unlikely Tale of Chase and Finnegan*. She lives near Chicago, Illinois, with her family.

Kao Kalia Yang is an award-winning Hmong American author of books for adults and children. Her genre-crossing books center Hmong and refugee families and speak to the importance of peace, justice, and communal care. Yang holds an honorary doctorate of humane letters from Carleton College and is a Guggenheim Fellow in nonfiction.

Suggested Further Reading

Anta, Julio, and Jacoby Salcedo. *Frontera*. HarperAlley, 2023.

Arnold, Marie. *I Rise*. Versify, 2022.

Buford, Candace. *Kneel*. Inkyard, 2021.

Medina, Tony. *I Am Alfonso Jones*. Illustrated by Stacey Robinson and John Jennings. Tu Books, 2017.

Mendoza, Paola, and Abby Sher. *Sanctuary*. G. P. Putnam's Sons, 2020.

Nelson, Marilyn. *A Wreath for Emmett Till*. Houghton Mifflin, 2005.

Rankine, Claudia. *Citizen: An American Lyric*. Graywolf, 2014.

Reed, Christina Hammonds. *The Black Kids*. Simon & Schuster BFYR, 2020.

Tyner, Artika R. *Reimagining Police: The Future of Public Safety*. Twenty-First Century Books, 2024.

Yoo, Paula. *Rising from the Ashes: Los Angeles, 1992. Edward Jae Song Lee, Latasha Harlins, Rodney King, and a City on Fire*. Norton, 2024.

Permissions

"Speaking in the Silence" © 2026 by Carolyn Holbrook

"No Kinda Right" © 2026 by Nikki Grimes

"The Human Hand Has 27 Bones" © 2026 by Sun Yung Shin

"Last Words" © 2026 by D. R. Bernstrom

"I Don't Know Where He Kept His Gun, with Headlines" © 2026 by Laura Ruby

"Breath Under Water" © 2026 by Kao Kalia Yang

"They tried to bury the neighborhood" © 2026 by Ty Chapman

"See You Tomorrow" © 2026 by Erin Entrada Kelly

Ada Limón, "A New National Anthem" from *The Carrying*. Copyright © 2018 by Ada Limón. Reprinted with the permission of The Permissions Company LLC on behalf of Milkweed Editions, milkweed.org.

"This Has Always Been Our Active Shooter Drill" Copyright © 2018 by Jason Reynolds. Originally published in Poem-a-Day on July 31, 2018, by the Academy of American Poets.

Entire Text from CAN WE PLEASE GIVE THE POLICE DEPARTMENT TO THE GRANDMOTHERS? by Junauda Petrus, text copyright © 2023 by Junauda Petrus. Used by permission of Dutton Children's Books, an imprint of Penguin Young Readers Group, a division of Penguin Random House LLC. All rights reserved.

"Church" © 2026 by Ari Tison

"Without Context" © 2026 by Padma Venkatraman

"Saturday Morning on 3rd and Lenora" © 2026 by Tae Keller

"This Year, 29 Anti-Trans Bills Became Law" © 2026 by Ollie Schminkey

"Uvalde Villain-elle" © 2026 by K. A. Holt

"Watershed (A Scene from the Very Near Future)" © 2026 by Kyle Tran Myhre

"Designed for Off the Chain" *Call & Response Gorget*" © 2025 by Douglas Kearney. Originally published in *I Imagine I Been Science Fiction Always*.

"8 (9)" © 2011 by Bao Phi. Originally published in *Sông I Sing*.

"The Policeman" © 2026 by Jasmine Warga

for minneapolis —A.T.

To the people, their power, and their endless capacity for compassion —T.C.

I would like to dedicate this book to my family. I would also like to dedicate this book to the spirit of community and courage needed to overcome tyranny and despair in our life and times. —D.D.

Zest Books™
An imprint of Lerner Publishing Group, Inc.
241 First Avenue North
Minneapolis, MN 55401 USA

For reading levels and more information, look up this title at www.lernerbooks.com.
Visit us at zestbooks.net.

Image credits: Nancy Hoyt Belcher/Alamy, pp. 18–19; Riddhish Chakraborty/Getty Images, pp. 24–25; Scott Takushi/MediaNews Group/St. Paul Pioneer Press via Getty Images, pp. 40–41. Design element: Olga Thelavart/Unsplash.

Main body text set in Futura Std. Typeface provided by Adobe Systems.
The illustrations in this book were created with paper, paint, ink, love, and care.

Library of Congress Cataloging-in-Publication Data

Names: Tison, Ari editor | Chapman, Ty editor | Davis, Damon illustrator
Title: Witness : poems to address the past, present, and future of policing / edited by Ari Tison and Ty Chapman ; illustrations by Damon Davis.
Description: Minneapolis : Zest Books, [2026] | Includes bibliographical references. | Audience: Ages 13–18 | Audience: Grades 10–12 | Summary: "A powerful poetry anthology from a multifaceted chorus of voices explores a range of experiences and emotions related to policing. This book gives readers an opportunity to reflect, to discuss, and above all, to witness" —Provided by publisher.
Identifiers: LCCN 2025047265 (print) | LCCN 2025047266 (ebook) | ISBN 9798765647240 library binding | ISBN 9798765659625 epub
Subjects: LCSH: Police—United States—Poetry | Law enforcement—United States—Poetry | American poetry—21st century | Young adult poetry, American | LCGFT: Poetry
Classification: LCC PS595.P632 W58 2026 (print) | LCC PS595.P632 (ebook)

LC record available at https://lccn.loc.gov/2025047265
LC ebook record available at https://lccn.loc.gov/2025047266

Manufactured in Guang Dong, China, by Dream Colour Printing
1-1010990-53154-2/16/2026